Medical School Interview Guide

Matthew Brutsché

Edited by Leslie Michaelis

www.medicalschoolinterviewguide.com

Cover Design by Leslie Michaelis

Library of Congress Cataloging-in-Publication Data

Brutsché, Matthew, edited by: Leslie Michaelis
    Medical School Interview Guide / Matthew Brutsché
    ISBN: 144-9-920-055
    EAN: 9-7814-49920-050

First Edition: September 2008
Second Edition: April 2010

TABLE OF CONTENTS

Congratulations! You've done it!

You have followed a path riddled with countless hours of studying and memorizing facts, innumerable lecture sessions, and untold expense in anticipation of applying to medical school. Now, you are closer than ever to your goal.

The next challenge you face is one most graduates find daunting: that all-important interview for medical school. Few prospective students worry about their medical school interviews until they are imminent. In fact, most individuals likely will have an interview scheduled before they refer to this guide. Provided you adhere to the program described in this manual, however, you will be better prepared for your interview than nearly all of your competitors.

Be ready to challenge yourself by following the steps found in the upcoming chapters. Some of the tactics described here are well-recognized interview techniques, while others are proven sales methods. By mastering these skills, you will convince interviewers you are the ideal candidate for their school.

As you read this manual, keep the following in mind:

❑ Understanding abstract concepts is no substitute for firsthand experience. Though the book presents many ideas, accomplishment comes from putting principles into practice.

❑ As concepts are presented, try to identify how each relates to your specific goals. Take individual suggestions personally. After all, this process is entirely about you.

❑ Preparing for your interview is a long and arduous process, but the enthusiasm for success you have already demonstrated offers great rewards for your effort.

Keep an eye out for this symbol. This appears where you will have work to do.

Now, let's get to it!

Chapter 1

Overview of Objectives

You have probably known for some time now that you would have to eventually suffer through the awkwardness of interviewing for medical school. As the prospect of your first interview draws near, your anxiety about it is likely now at an all-time high. If you weren't in the least bit anxious, it would be improbable that you would be reading this book.

The formality of the medical school interview might seem superfluous. After all, your grades and your application say everything there is to know about your candidacy as a medical student. Right? What could a complete stranger (or, perish the thought, a panel of strangers) learn in an hour that would convince them that your desire to attend their institution is sincere?

The answer is: **plenty.** The medical school interview is the forum in which you will be allowed to prove your dedication to your academic career, your integrity as a member of the medical community, and the accuracy of your application as an assessment of your potential as a medical student.

The interviewer or interviewers will ask a myriad of questions pertaining to your academic history, your personal endeavors outside of school, your beliefs, and your views about the medical profession as a whole. When all is said and done, however, the pivotal question in your interview will be: Why are you pursuing a degree in medicine?

Although on the surface this may appear quite obvious, nearly every question put to you will be, in some fashion or other, an attempt to give the interview panel an opportunity to learn your reasons for attending their school and discerning whether your reasons make you an appropriate candidate for study at their institution. Consequently, your interview must demonstrate professionalism, determination, and integrity. The following chapters are designed to arm you with the tools necessary to interview competently and confidently, preparing you for the moments when you are facing the individuals who hold the keys to your career in medicine.

Confidence comes most easily when the topic is one the speaker knows well. By researching many medical specialties, you will be able to knowledgeably enter the discussion of your future in medicine. In Chapter 2 of this book, you will explore the medical fields of most interest to you. When your research is complete, you will use your knowledge to formulate opinions about the medical profession as a whole, clearly state the goals you want to achieve, and identify the steps required to reach your career objectives.

As you will discover, the greatest resource available to you during the exploration of your interests will be people; medical specialists you may already know, persons with whom you work, friends, family, fellow students, and even their associates, can provide you with invaluable assistance in your quest to enter the medical profession. Chapter 3, you will identify the people within your circle of influence who can best benefit your aims.

After you have selected several fields of interest and composed a list of contacts within those fields, you will conduct brief informational interviews with medical professionals (Chapters 4 & 5). The primary objective of informational interviews will be to learn from knowledgeable sources the specifics of working in different medical disciplines, allowing you to evaluate the features of each that appeal to you most. Secondarily, you will have your first opportunities to practice techniques for managing dialogue in a formal setting.

Next, Chapter 6 will give you an overview of the usual formats for medical school admission interviews and tips for giving your best performance during each type of interview.

The final steps in preparing for your interview are persistent practice. Conducting mock interviews will give your presentation a conversational polish and fluidity, enhancing the image of professionalism you intend to project. Methods for conducting mock interviews are outlined extensively in Chapters 7, 8 & 9.

Once you have completed the tasks outlined in this book, you will have a better understanding of the type of doctor you would like to be. You will be able to assess your academic and professional career goals. You will have practiced your interview skills under various conditions so that you exude confidence during your medical school interview.

Let's just summarize the steps you will follow:

1. Explore the options available to you. These include not only which medical schools you might attend, but also the many specialties you might pursue as your studies progress.

2. Use your circle of influence to gain more information about the field of medicine.

3. Interview as many medical professionals as you can arrange to meet.

4. Learn about medical school interviews.

5. Practice for the medical school interview with at least two mock interviews.

Chapter 2

Exploring Your Options

Test scores, grades, and affiliations have given you an opportunity to be considered for medical school, but they will only get you the interview. Now, you must demonstrate why you are the right candidate.

To present a dynamic interview, you must demonstrate thoughtfulness, determination, maturity, and strength to your interviewers. These are subjective qualities that can be difficult to convey to people who do not know you well. Ensuring your interview translates these qualities about you is done by stating clearly to yourself that you know what you want. When you internalize the truth of your goals initially to yourself, you are in a much better position to translate your certainty to others.

Those individuals who know what they want are perceived as strong, and having direction can illustrate the necessary level of commitment and interest. Therefore, the first step is to establish a clear goal. It is not enough to want to become a doctor. All of your competitors want to be doctors, too. Your interviewers naturally will assume this. Why else would you be interviewing for medical school?

Establishing a goal requires a great deal of introspection on your earnest desires. You will have to ask yourself potentially difficult questions about your reasons for attending medical school. What do you hope to get out of your education? What career or careers do you think will be most fulfilling? How do you define personal success? The time to begin asking these questions is while you have the resources to perform informal research and have the motivation to identify a career path.

In this chapter, you will find some straightforward methods for synthesizing a goal from the intersection of your wants and the vast array of possibilities. The process outlined here will become a resource to which you can refer, regardless of where you are in your career. Whenever you find a new field of interest, need direction, or want to validate your progress, use these techniques to guide you toward your destination. Enter into this process with an open mind and you might just learn something you didn't know!

Discover What You Want

Take a moment to stand back from the immediate task of getting into medical school and try to identify just what medical school will ultimately help you to accomplish. Maybe you desire the implied independence of a small practice. Perhaps the prestige and responsibility embodied in the title Chief of Surgery holds some allure for you.

Deciphering what motivates you may be overwhelming at first. There are many wants you have to wade through to find the fundamental forces that drive you. However, getting at the core of your wants is essential to establishing goals. In this section, you are going to list and prioritize your wants very broadly. Later, you will compare this list against the attributes of potential career paths in order to establish a goal statement. The goal statement will be the focus around which your interview responses will revolve when the time comes.

Step 1. List as many things as you can in ten minutes that you think you want. Each response should be only a few words at most (e.g., financial security, help the mentally ill, a family, to learn a language, to write a book, etc.). They do not have to be related to your career, simply something you hope your future holds. Nothing is off limits. The importance of honesty cannot be over-emphasized. Do not list what you think you should want, only list what you truly desire.

Step 2. Now, look closely over your list and circle the ten things that are most important to you. Notice any trends? When items in your list appear similar to several others, a core need is presenting itself. See if you can identify any patterns in your responses. If you are truly stumped, find someone you believe is both analytical and reflective to review your list and give you their impressions. Perhaps they will identify something you didn't even recognize about yourself.

Step 3. Make a statement that attempts to encompass all of the things in your top ten without listing each item individually. This step may appear difficult if your top ten includes things like "a classic Harley" and "find my true love," but with a bit of patience and self-analysis, it can be done. Try to synthesize your list into your core needs (for example, security, freedom, acclaim).

Goal Statement

For now, this sentence comprises what is required for you to reach personal success. In Chapter 6, you will formulate a more specific goal statement related to your pursuit of a medical degree. Before you can do so, however, you will need more information.

Brainstorm the Possibilities

You may be uncertain about your academic path, but exploring options will give you an edge over other candidates. Most qualified applicants will have researched the different medical disciplines and envisioned themselves in various professional roles before applying to school. If you have already settled on a course of study, exploring alternatives will give you more insight into your chosen field and allow you to qualify the coursework available at the institution with which you are interviewing.

Let's start with a good brainstorming session. Using the template below, list the medical disciplines with which you are interested or at least familiar, noting your level of interest in each. If your goal is to attend medical school in pursuit of a career in a related field, such as epidemiology or medical equipment sales, make a list of those fields, too. You may continue this list further on a separate sheet of paper if you run out of room.

Professional Interests

1. **Field/Job Title:**

   Very Interested   Somewhat Interested   Mildly Interested

2. **Field/Job Title:**

   Very Interested   Somewhat Interested   Mildly Interested

3. **Field/Job Title:**

   Very Interested   Somewhat Interested   Mildly Interested

4. **Field/Job Title:**

   Very Interested   Somewhat Interested   Mildly Interested

5. **Field/Job Title:**

   Very Interested   Somewhat Interested   Mildly Interested

6. **Field/Job Title:**

   Very Interested   Somewhat Interested   Mildly Interested

7. **Field/Job Title:**

   Very Interested   Somewhat Interested   Mildly Interested

8. **Field/Job Title:**

   Very Interested   Somewhat Interested   Mildly Interested

9. **Field/Job Title:**

Very Interested   Somewhat Interested   Mildly Interested

10. **Field/Job Title:**

Very Interested   Somewhat Interested   Mildly Interested

If you are like many and a little curious about a lot of things, then you may have 20 or more different areas of interest. Great job! This will be a good place to begin. If you don't have a list of at least 10, write down some specialties with which you are at least acquainted. The areas included in your list do not even have to be fields that you would seriously consider practicing; they only need to be those you cannot yet eliminate.

"What's so great about being a...?"

At least a few of the professions you listed above appear very attractive as possible career futures. The next exercise is designed to help you examine why. You will want to reference your list of wants and compare how each profession might satisfy them as you go.

Begin by keeping a notebook or a text file with a section for each field of study (your notebook will come in handy later when you begin informational interviews, so keep it close). Next, use the template below to write a brief statement at the head of every section that summarizes why you are interested in each field of medicine. Maybe you met an engaging doctor who works in the field, or perhaps you read something mesmerizing about that area's technological advances. If you have your heart set on Chief of Surgery, then include words to that affect in your statement. Don't worry about supplying a narrative at this point.

Field/Job Title:

I am interested in this because...

Wants this may satisfy:

Necessary qualifications:

Do I have those qualifications?

What do I need to do to become qualified?

Much of the basic research needed to answer the questions above can be done on your own. Use your resources wisely and stick to credible sources. Utilize local medical associations and organizations when it is appropriate. Requirements for education and experience can be found by searching medical job posts online or consulting medical employment services. If you find that you are missing a key undergraduate class, for example, you will want to fill in the gap. Taking steps to address any shortcoming in your qualifications early will go a long way toward showing interviewers that you are dedicated.

The synopses you create should give you a broad overview of your interests and create an outline for the research you will do in following chapters. Investigation into specific occupations may change your mind about a specialty you once believed to be promising. Likewise, you may discover that other professions would better provide what you seek.

Before you can make a sound choice about your course of study, you need information about what each occupation entails. Right now, your perspective about your future in medicine is limited because you have not yet experienced life as a doctor. To compensate for a lack of personal experience, however, you can learn from the experiences of others. This is where informational interviewing comes in particularly useful. Not only will you glean invaluable insights about prospective career paths, you will get your first opportunities to practice the interviewing techniques from Chapter 5. It may be difficult to find people who would be willing to spare time out of their days to help you, however. In the next chapter, your task is to look to people within your circle of influence for help.

Chapter 3

Circle of Influence

As you progress through this book, it will become more apparent that the more information you have about the academic and professional careers you have laid out for yourself, the more confident you will be about the decisions you have made to pursue them. In this chapter, you are going to take a break from focusing on your goals and direct your attention to one of the greatest resources of information you have at your disposal: your circle of influence.

Define your circle of influence as the group of people to whom you are connected—your parents, best friends, professors, coworkers. The diagram on the next page visually represents your circle of influence. It is said that there are "six degrees of separation" between any two people. If each person is simply one "connection" away from another, then we are all only six connections away from everyone on Earth.

Place yourself in the middle of the circle and identify the people you know as part of the diagram. The people closest to you in the circle are the strongest relationships while people furthest out are connected less strongly.

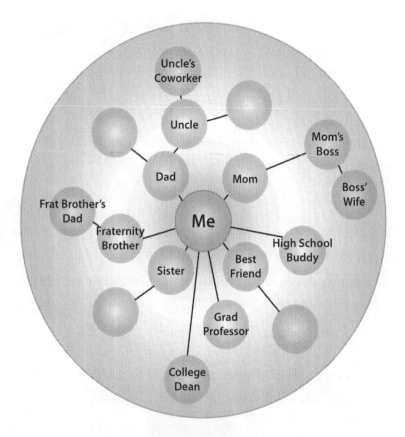

Circle of Influence

Choose any single person in your diagram and recognize that they have their own circle of influence. Through the connection to the person in your circle, you are now connected to a vast number of people whom you have never even met! It doesn't matter where any one person is positioned in your circle; you can reach them all. Each of these people is someone you can affect and who can have an impact on you. You begin to notice how powerful your circle of influence can be.

There is a large body of evidence to indicate that people who master the art of networking have a wider choice of job opportunities, suffer less from unemployment, and even receive better pay than their counterpart with exactly the same skill set and work experience. Your connections to people are just as important as technical knowledge when it comes to success in your chosen field. Not only do these connections have the potential to provide you with opportunities for internship and employment, but they can open you up to a wealth of knowledge you do not currently possess, knowledge crucial to a successful medical school interview and essential in determining your academic career goals. You need to know what can only be gained by experience: how to interact with people much like your interviewers.

When you speak about your interest in medicine, your interviewers should hear the perspective of sympathetic understanding. Since it is not possible for you to have had your own experiences, the easiest way to gain this understanding is to draw on the experiences of others. Even if you are personally acquainted with few, if any, medical professionals, you are likely connected to someone who is. Ask yourself if entering medical school is important enough for you to seek out people close to you who know someone in the world of medicine?

The method you will use to approach those within your circle should be easy and non-confrontational, since these are people you already know. Simply ask the people within your circle if they know anyone in the medical industry willing to spare a few minutes educating you about what he or she does. Do they personally know any nurses, doctors, or of any opportunities that might help you identify medical industry professionals who would be available to speak with you for 20 minutes? That's it. As you make your request, clarify that you are preparing for medical school interviews, not selling anything or asking for more than insights on the medical profession. Obviously, the approach you would use in contacting your mother will be quite different from the one you would use to contact Dr. Smith!

Many people disdain the sales profession for a number of valid reasons, primarily because pushy people can be unpleasant. Many people could never imagine a career in sales. You are not being asked to become a pushy salesperson. You need not waste your time reading sales literature, but you do need to recognize that sales techniques work. Sales methods have their place in this world.

When used correctly, effective networking techniques will create partners who can help you accomplish more than you can alone. Once mastered, networking is a tool you will keep in your back pocket as you move through life. Your ability to network will pay off in the future, especially when you open your own office and need patient referrals!

"I Wouldn't Want to Impose"

Maybe you don't feel comfortable asking those in your circle to get you in touch with their contacts in medicine. You will, of course, be more comfortable asking friends and family for assistance in reaching doctors, and they will be more honest with you. Perhaps you are shy or have a difficult time approaching people with whom you are not particularly close. Shyness is an emotionally difficult barrier to overcome in many aspects of your life, but if you begin by approaching people in the center of your circle (the people closest to you) and work your way methodically out, eventually you will discover that the neighbor you have met only in passing may be just as willing to help you with your pursuit of medical school as your brother.

Before you dismiss this opportunity, consider how much more prepared you will be for your medical school interview by accessing this pivotal resource. Primarily, your understanding of the challenges faced by professionals in the field will add sophistication to the responses you give during the interview. Your willingness to pursue an enhanced understanding of your chosen profession also demonstrates dedication to your education. How thoroughly you have prepared will be apparent. Secondarily, you gain exposure to people who are similar to your potential interviewers and become acclimated to speaking in a formal environment, thus reducing the awkwardness typically associated with the interview process. This sounds like a counter-intuitive way to become comfortable with interviews, but it works. The more practice you have asking and answering questions related to your interest in medicine, the more natural your responses to interview questions will become. Talking with doctors will be your single most powerful tool in preparation for your interview.

Some people you approach will hesitate to give you their contacts if they don't fully trust your intentions. With practice and careful listening to the responses your receive, you will become more adept at asking each successive person for their assistance because you will become more sensitive to what they may find offensive. You will also discover that there are many people close to you willing to bend over backwards to offer you support!

Tapping Your Network

To begin exploring your network, use the worksheet on the next page to list the people you know. List everyone. Although creating such a list may sound like an ominous task, you can start with 10 of your closest family members, friends, office colleagues, or college associates. Initiating this process with family members and close friends is common. In fact, the top spots on the list of people in your circle of influence will probably be relatives. Family members can be among your greatest assets. If you don't have family support, though, do not be discouraged. You can start with people with whom you feel most comfortable. What is important is to start developing contacts. If you do not make lists, you likely will get lost later, so use whatever method you can to keep this information organized.

My Circle of Influence

You may have to get creative in identifying your circle of influence. Begin looking for people who may not be doctors but who are in daily contact with doctors. For example, do you or anyone in your circle of influence know anyone who sells medical equipment, pharmaceuticals, or medical supplies? Do you know anyone who knows a nurse? Anyone who works at a hospital or whose clients include those in the medical profession is a viable candidate to contact. Look for any possible connection that will get you to closer to a doctor.

Family

Friends

Teachers

Coworkers

Acquaintances

Organizations, affiliations, clubs

Doctors or nurses I know

After you have made your way through the list of people and have identified all the possible leads, place a check next to the names of contacts who are themselves medical professionals or are likely to have direct access to someone in the medical field. Don't hesitate to revisit this list and expand it so that you have 15 to 20 strong connections to medical professionals. Essentially, you are trying to get to know the people your people know. Some people know a lot of people, others not so many. Your goal is to work with these people to discover the ones who can help you. Someone's best friend is a doctor. That person may have the influence to get his best friend to meet with you for 20 minutes.

"I just don't know anyone!"

If your resources run dry, you must be willing to do whatever it takes to achieve this task. After identifying your fields of interest in Chapter 2, you may resort to grabbing the telephone book, researching a number of physicians in your field of choice, and directly calling doctor's offices. This is referred to as a cold call. Cold calls are acceptable, too! You can call anyone you want, describe your situation, and ask to meet with them for 20 minutes to discuss their career. Explain that you are preparing for medical school and would like to learn more about their profession. You may also tell them that you would have preferred to meet with people you know, but you don't know any doctors. This might make them more sympathetic to your plight. The number of people who will speak with you if you gently ask is impressive. Simply be honest, state what you want, and be present if they give you their time.

When you first ask members in your inner circle of influence if they will help introduce you to doctors, they may not remember or know anyone to whom they can refer you immediately. Check back with them periodically as they may encounter new people who may fit your needs. Be sure to ask the people on your list to keep you in mind if they meet someone in the medical field or if they learn that any of their contacts know medical professionals. Contact the people in your circle of influence once every two weeks and ask if they have identified anyone in the medical field who can assist you. Make this request in any way you feel comfortable. Ask your contacts directly, or simply mention that you are still looking for doctors to meet. By exercising this type of networking skill, you raise awareness for your cause. The longer your contacts go without communicating with you, the less aware they will be that you still need their assistance.

"Great! I have long list. Now What?"

In short, you are going to prepare for your interview, by interviewing. Set up an appointment to meet with each of the medical professionals on your list for exactly 20 minutes. State that you are preparing for medical school interviews and would like more information about what your contact does. Do not send the request in a mass e-mail message. Your request is a very personal one, so address each request personally. And remember, this is training—a sort-of medical school interview boot camp—so be professional.

Once you establish appointments with a medical professional, always be cognizant of your contacts' time and energy. Your time is not important—your contact's time is very important. It should be taken seriously. Your future depends on it! If you make appointments and do not keep them or arrive to your appointments late, you should think twice about attending medical school. After all, who would be likely to recommend you for a residency or permanent position if you are late or inconsiderate of their valuable time?

Before you conduct your first interview, read Chapters 4 and 5 thoroughly, so that you are prepared for your meeting. After reading these chapters you should have a clear understanding of what an informational interview is and how to conduct one efficiently.

Chapter 4

Informational Interviews

You can learn in many ways: from books, lectures, and visual presentations. While these methods can be effective in acquiring knowledge about history or biology, in the "people business" there are no substitutes for direct interaction and firsthand experience. Mediators, psychologists, and corporate negotiators deal competently with some of the most precarious personal interactions nearly every day. It is their ability to actively listen that makes them so skilled at their occupations. They hear not only what their clients are saying, but also the meaning that lies behind what is being said.

Although nearly every person believes he/she is a good listener (after all, we've been listening our entire lives), the truth is, most of us aren't. But we can all learn to listen well. You are going to use informational interviews to practice your listening skills. When you learn to actively listen to the questions posed during your medical school interview, your answers will become more direct and coherent. You will be less likely to ramble or give inappropriate responses, because you will understand what your interviewers are really trying to find out about you.

Great Rewards

Not everyone who reads this guide will invest the time and effort required to follow through the steps outlined in this chapter and the next, but the benefits of doing so are enormous.

> *If you get nothing else out of this text, conducting informational interviews is the single most beneficial way for you to prepare for your medical school interview.*

Communicating with medical professionals will give you insight into how others have dealt with their own successes and failures. Some of the people you meet will have pursued and accomplished personal aspirations to position themselves in a place of great prestige, but, like most of us, they had to combat their personal insecurities and fears in order to achieve their goals. Even the most well-regarded surgeons in the best hospitals in the world struggled with career choices at one time or another. Whether their conflict came as a result of a lack of academic accomplishment, conflict with superiors and subordinates, overcoming the inevitable aggravations associated with navigating the political environment of an administrative body, or coming to terms with short-term failure, every successful individual has had to overcome any number of personal hurdles to gain accomplishment. With skillful listening and probing, you will find that nearly every person you interview is quite willing to share the highs and lows associated with their success.

The insights and experiences of these experts may even shape and influence your own medical career. Your interview subjects may divulge professional tips and shortcuts they have discovered. Often, you will unveil the motivation behind their career goals. You will be surprised at how many people became doctors because of outside influence rather than a life calling.

The greatest benefit of practicing your listening skills through informational interviewing is that gradually you will become immune to the discomfort most people suffer during interviews. Think about a nervous speaker who doesn't often talk in front of large groups. Such speakers are anxious and stumble, offering lackluster presentations, leaving  their audiences more focused on the speaker's discomfort than the material covered. It happens all of the time. Would you have the confidence and comfort level to present your best self if you were being interviewed right now? Probably not.

During interviews and public speaking, your body feels threatened by the focused attention of others, sensing there may be either emotional or physical danger. The only cure for such discomfort is through desensitization. If you repeatedly put yourself in situations where the attention of others meets with no real danger, eventually your body stops sending the signal that you are being threatened, allowing you to relax. Once you are at your ease, your confidence and competence become immediately apparent. Informational interviews are a convenient method for desensitization.

This process will change you. When you finish you will have a much broader perspective about medicine than when you started. And most certainly one of the questions the interviewers at your prospective school will ask themselves is whether you really understand and appreciate the demands of becoming a physician. Their motivation is quite straightforward: they want their students graduate, because losing enrollees prior to graduation is a significant loss of revenue to the school. If you sit in front of an interviewer and say, "I have always wanted to be a doctor so I am going to go to medical school," the interviewer might assume that you have not invested sufficient time toward deciding your career goal. On the other hand, if you say, "I have spoken with 23 doctors, 15 nurses, and several others in the medical industry and have decided, after careful consideration, that being a doctor is the right choice for me," the interviewer will be more assured of your career choice. Neither statement is right or wrong, but the second speaks to the schools' interest as well as your own.

Informational interviews can also give you an idea of what a medical school is like on the inside. That understanding will help identify you as the type of student the school is seeking. In fact, securing informational interviews with individuals at medical schools is a wonderful way to begin. University staff and students can answer your questions about their true impressions of the school and what it has to offer. With the insight you've gained from your informational interviews, you will be more prepared to communicate naturally with those who are conducting your medical school interview.

Will talking with doctors or other medical professionals will help you answer the "tough" ethical questions you may are likely to be asked during your medical school interview? The truth is that it may not. Responses to ethical dilemmas are very personal, and another's insights may not alter your own beliefs. But if you ask doctors enough questions about ethics and other challenges they face, you will acquire a deeper understanding of the issues doctors encounter every day. This understanding will inevitably make your responses to personal questions more thoughtful, because your formulation of them will draw upon the views and experiences of a range of others as well as your own. You will have done the groundwork to relate to your interviewers on their level.

Make the Appointment

Schedule twenty-minute appointments with the medical contacts from the list you created in Chapter 3. Explain that you are a prospective medical student and ask if they can spare twenty minutes to speak with you about their professional experiences. You may have to be persistent in getting an appointment scheduled, so be prepared to make follow-up calls. Persistent does not mean

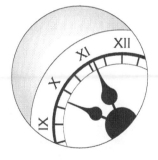

annoying. If a contact does not return several of your calls, they are likely very busy, so don't leave innumerable voice mail messages or send an e-mail every day until they respond. If you eventually receive a response after such a bombardment, it is not likely to be a favorable one.

Try to arrange appointments with professionals both in the fields in which you are very interested and in areas that seem less appealing. An interview that confirms the reasons why a particular field doesn't suit you can be just as informative as one in which you have a great interest. Knowing the specifics of what professions do and do not appeal to you can help put you right on track for your future. Refer to the list of professional interest you made in Chapter 2.

Remember to be considerate of your contacts' time by keeping your request brief and topical. Refer often to the informational interview techniques in Chapter 5.

Before the Interview

Preparing for an informational interview is similar to preparing for a medical school interview. You will want to know something about the person with whom you are interviewing and what information will be covered during the interview. Your questions should be well formulated ahead of time to ensure the interview doesn't lag.

Begin by doing a bit of background research. First, imagine you are applying for the job of everyone you interview. What will be expected of you: the daily tasks of the job, the educational requirements, work conditions and schedule? What are the primary sub-specialties within that field? Have any recent or major medical advancements been made in that field? How much supervision or supervising is necessary in this position? Would you work as part of a team or are you generally left to your own devices? Defining your subject's role is the focus of the informational interview process. Your research of these questions prior to the interview will help you ask better questions. You will learn more during the interview and respond more effectively as it progresses.

Once you have a firm understanding of what the professional you will be interviewing does, formulate a list of open-ended questions for them to answer. Open-ended means that the answer to the question will require the subject to respond with more than "yes" or "no". For example, avoid questions, such as, "Do you like hours that you keep?" Instead, you could ask, "How do the hours that you work allow you time for personal pursuits?" Your questions should be designed to get your subject to elaborate and expound, not just give a simple response. The more your subject speaks, the more you will glean about what you really want to know: their feelings and perspective about what they do.

Sample Informational Interview Questions

1. Tell me about being a doctor or medical professional?

2. What do you enjoy most about what you do?

3. What exactly are your responsibilities in this role?

4. How did you get this position?

5. Is this job your ultimate goal, or do you have plans to move into a different role in your career?

6. Why did medicine appeal to you in the first place?

7. How do you make a difference in peoples lives? Is it what you thought it would be when you were a student?

8. What is the best part of your job? What is the worst?

9. Are you for or against universal health care? Why or why not?

10. How do you feel you could have been better prepared by your education for the career you chose?

11. How has the medical industry has changed since you started?

12. What skills do you think students coming out of medical school should possess to take on the problems that we face today?

13. Tell me about your career path. How did you get achieve the position you have today?

14. What do you think is the greatest challenge facing future medical professionals?

15. What are you most proud of in your medical career?

16. Which jobs could you have had with your education that you rejected outright? Why?

17. If you could get other people to understand one thing about your job that they seem to miss, what would it be?

18. What ethical questions do people in your profession face? How do you deal with the grey areas that you come across?

19. What events occur during your routine that make you nervous or uneasy?

Etiquette

Show your interview subject the respect they deserve for taking the time to help you. Arrive promptly at your interview, well-dress and clean. Since the interview is informal, a suit is not necessarily required in all cases, but be aware of the environment into which you will be walking. There are very few circumstances under which sneakers and shorts will be taken seriously. After your interview, thank your host and shake their hand. Send a sincere note or e-mail a day or so later to express your gratitude. Simple courtesies can go a long way toward establishing a connection with your interview subject. Who knows when and under what circumstances you may meet again?

In the next chapter you will learn specific techniques for interviewing that will help you learn to listen to the responses you receive to your questions. After each interview, review your list of questions and revise them if they did not produce the results for which you had hoped.

Chapter 5

Informational Interview Techniques

This chapter summarizes the fundamental strategies for conducting informational interviews in a way that will help you accomplish two simple goals: (1) become more comfortable with the interview environment, and (2) investigate professions in which you have a sincere interest. These secondary goals serve as a foundation for your primary goal, securing a place in medical school. As you interview doctors and medical professionals, always keep in mind that the techniques outlined here are designed to aid you in this pursuit.

By taking on the role of the interviewer, you will begin to notice parallels between the questions you are asking and those you will face in your medical school interviews. Reflect on the answers you obtain from your interview subjects to see how their responses reflect their attitudes about their work. Is the impression you receive from their answers a favorable one? How would a slightly reworded response have given you a more positive impression? Take care to note your perceptions after each interview.

This Is For You, Not About You

Understand one thing clearly: this process is not about you, it is about the subject. The professionals you interview have something you don't have—experience. Some interviewee will have exactly the type of experience you'd like to gain. Don't waste time talking about yourself. No offense meant to you, but you really do not have anything meaningful to contribute at this point, and your relevance to your subjects' lives is minimal in comparison to their relevance to yours!

People become fond of those with whom they have an opportunity to speak about themselves or about things that they know. So, the more questions you ask and the more you listen, the more likely those you interview will support your endeavors. On the other hand, the more you talk about yourself, the more they will dislike you. Learning to influence how others perceive you can only bring positive outcomes during your medical school interview and throughout your life.

Rigorously Prepare

Laying the proper groundwork will not only make your informational interviews go smoothly, but prepare you for every aspect of your medical school interview. Proper preparation means practicing interview questions, formalizing the practice by participating in mock interviews, and increasing your knowledge about your potential path through medical school. Although there is always room for innovation, most likely you will not be recreating the wheel on your journey. Gather as much general information as you can about your host's profession before you meet, then construct several questions only someone in that profession could answer. Preparation speaks volumes about your dedication to the subject at hand.

During informational interviews, you will explore the fields in which you are most interested. As you prepare, imagine you will be taking the place of the doctor you interview. What would you need to know? Which of his or her insights would you want to explore? What does a person in this position do all day? Obtaining insight into the role that doctors play is at the center of the informational interview process.

Confirmation of interesting facts or speculation is also a great way to assess the accuracy of the research you have done. For example, you may find that a controversial consumer issue you encountered during your preliminary research, such as the possible link between vaccines and autism, is a typical concern for most pediatricians. On the other hand, you may discover that there is a lively debate among your interviewee's colleagues on this very topic and that there may be policy changes in the near future. A topical question can give you details about your potential profession and solidly establish that your interest in your host's field is sincere.

The more organized your thoughts, the more influence you will have. Informational interviews develop strong interpersonal skills that can have powerful effects on people. With correct application and practice, you will be able to gain valuable information. The better prepared you are before the interview, the more readily you will be able to determine when a gem of knowledge is being passed on to you.

Get Personal

You are attempting to establish a personal relationship with your subject. Do not attempt to complete these interviews over the telephone. The informational interviews must be conducted in person. You will not interview for medical school via the telephone or e-mail, so only in-person interviews will be good practice. If talking to someone face-to-face makes you uncomfortable, you need the practice most of all.

After several questions concerning your host's profession during the interview, endeavor to ask ones concerning their personal feelings and experiences. One of the best ways to do this is by inquiring about qualifications. As an example, you may say, "I found quite a bit of information regarding the educational requirements necessary for a position such as yours. Tell me about the path you took to reach this point." After the medical professional answers, you may follow-up with a question such as, "If you could go back, would you have done anything differently?" or, "What is the most important lesson you've learned in your career?"

Investigating how someone has achieved professional status is the shortest path to putting your subject at ease. After all, about what topic can anyone speak more knowledgeably than his or her history and perceptions? The conversation will become very personal to your host, as she will be speaking about her own experiences. Respect everything she says, regardless of your own personal beliefs.

There will be a time in your career that you will ask yourself how far you would like to go. What do you want to achieve and by when do you want to achieve it? You may have been asking yourself these questions already because these concerns are universal. Everyone struggles with internal questions about their future, though people rarely discuss them outside their inner circle. Speaking with 20 doctors or medical professionals will grant you insight into how these individuals found answers to their questions.

Look for the Patterns

If you talk with enough people, you will find a common thread through the responses you receive to your questions. For example, ask every informational interview candidate what they believed was the hardest part of becoming a doctor. You will surely get different answers, but there will be commonality between them all. At the very least, you will encounter ideas to which you can relate and harness yourself. Should you be asked during your medical school interview what you perceive will be the most difficult part of pursuing a career in medicine, you have sources from which to draw your conclusions.

Compare your subject's experiences with your interests to see if there are ties between what they perceive as positive aspects of their profession and your desired future. By asking probing questions about their lives, you will get a better feel for how their work may satisfy your own motivations.

Focus Your Interview With Questions

Generally, the person who is asking the questions is the person in control of the conversation. Guide the conversation with a balance of leading and open-ended questions. People respond to questions. Questioning your host during informational interviews is to your benefit because the more you listen, the more highly your host will think of you and the more important they will feel. Asking questions is a technique to get your subjects talking about themselves and their interests. Getting someone to speak openly about himself or herself is the secret to influencing people and their perception of you.

Great questions include things that interest you or speak to you on a personal level. Write down questions that get at exactly what each professional does. For example, "As the owner of your own practice, what percentage of your time do you dedicate to general business management?" Or even, "What is a typical day in the role of a cardiologist?

In a typical interview, you will often have to redirect the conversation to keep the interview subject focused on the questions at hand. As an accomplished and intelligent person, your host is likely also curious and has much to say on many topics. A common issue you will encounter during an interview will consequently be digression from the current topic. Generally, it is counterproductive to allow the interview to degenerate into a social conversation. Practice using questions to keep the interview focused.

When speaking with a doctor during an informational interview, you might have a conversation such as the following:

You: Thank you for speaking with me, Dr. Smith. I really appreciate your time. Would you mind if I asked you some questions about your experience in medicine and specifically what you do now?

Doctor: No, not at all. How long have you thought about going to medical school?

You: I've been interested in medicine since I watched a surgery on television when I was 15. May I ask what motivated you to study medicine?

Doctor: I was encouraged by my mother. And, as you know, mothers have a big influence on their children. Surgery, you say? Is that what you want to do?

You: Well, truthfully, I haven't decided. By the way, I wanted to ask how you came to select your area of specialty?

Did you notice something consistent throughout this brief conversation? In an interview of any kind it is important to never stop talking until you end with a question. Questions create a lot of discussion and give the impression you are curious and interested. Obviously, asking questions without responding to those asked of you would disrupt the rhythm of the conversation and create a negative impression. When you are asked a question, answer it straightforwardly, but avoid dominating the conversation; be wary not to waste valuable time with self-promotion. Your aim in this interview is to learn, not talk about yourself.

You may find it challenging at first to learn how to ask questions that prompt discussion. After all, you are putting the person with whom you are speaking on the spot, compelling them to take action. They will tell you what is important and why. The more you can get your subjects to talk, the more interested in you they will become. Liking someone is part of the bond that holds a network together. Try it on your friends. See if you can get your friends to talk 80% of the time just by asking questions. And every time you make a statement, try to end with an open-ended question.

Do not allow your interview subjects to digress from the topic of your inquiries toward information that may or may not be relevant. This is common when someone is not particularly focused on the question they have been asked or assume the question is headed in some other direction. Gently redirect the conversation back by rewording your question more explicitly. And, remember to avoid this pitfall in your medical school interview by listening carefully!

Avoid Discussions of Medical School Interviews

You won't gain very much by asking veteran physicians for insights concerning their own medical school interviews. Their histories and experiences are likely to differ from yours a great deal. Trying to shortcut to a template for approaching your upcoming interviews will likely have an undesirable outcome, since your responses will appear forced and insincere. It will be important that you are listening carefully to the questions you face during your interviews and not simply spitting back words and phrases you think worked for someone else.

Attempt, instead, to glean from your conversations with the myriad of doctors and medical workers you interview the characteristics of people who have achieved what you hope to attain. These characteristics obviously are indicative of the traits found in a good physician.

Remain Objective

When you encounter a moral question that has no right or wrong answer, form an opinion yourself, but attempt to understand how other people have answered it. Their experiences and backgrounds have helped shape their opinions. Listen carefully. They are privy to information you do not possess. Perhaps your view would be different with more relevant experiences of your own, so do not be dismissive or argumentative with your interview subject. If a topic appears too sensitive or likely to cause antagonism, simply move to the next line of questioning

Chapter 6

The Admissions Interview

In preparation for the admissions interview, you have now employed techniques that shape your ability to communicate your goals and intensions while giving you practice in presentation. You have obtained information about future career choices from people on the inside and received a brief immersion into the culture of medicine. The journey has transformed your intent to enter medical school into experiences you will use to enhance the quality of your projected image during the interview process. This chapter will familiarize you with the details of the medical school interview itself.

Working with Personalities

During your medical school interview, it will be important to be as genuine as possible. Interviewers expect honesty and truthfulness. Since you know you have no other reasonable choice than to be honest, use this knowledge to your advantage. Your ability to withstand judgment dur-

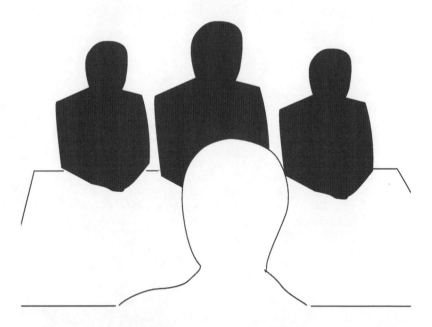

ing your admissions interview—a time when your anxiety will likely be high—is dependent on how confident you are about entering the world of medicine. Once you have researched the potential of various medical fields, conducted several informational interviews, and practiced mock interviews, your perspectives about medicine will become broader and deeper. And, your newfound perspective will be evident to those around you.

In the medical school interview, you must show you are determined, mature, thoughtful, and strong. Although your accomplishments, experience, and knowledge are important, they are not half as important to the interview process as the impression you make on the person or people who interview you. For that reason, it is essential you understand the interview process is not about you. The interview process is about what the interviewer thinks about you, and as a result, it revolves around the interviewer. Every interviewer will have their own personality. Predicting the personality of your interviewer is not possible, so the best you can do is go into the interview with a strategy to deal with the widest range of people.

It may be surprising for you to know that the people who conduct interviews really don't care all that much about you. Rarely is an interviewer interested in having you detail how perfect a pupil you are or how you intend to save the world one person at a time. Even if you are everything you claim, the simple fact is, shameless self-promotion probably won't get you to the top of your profession. In order to differentiate yourself from the rest of the pack, you must approach the interviewer in a way that is unique. With the experience you acquired in your informational interviews, you now have a perspective that distinguishes you from your competition, that of the interviewer. Most candidates will not approach the interview from the interviewer's viewpoint because they have not realized what can be gained by adopting this necessary perspective.

Understanding interviewers' motivations and the roles they occupy outside of the interview will help you make favorable impressions. The interviewer likely will be a member of the faculty or an alumnus and may perform their current function for a variety of personal and professional reasons (including a mandate by their college or universities to conduct interviews). It is also possible your interviewer has a personal agenda, such as, using their involvement in the academic interview process to support their political aims; they may even have volunteered for the assignment based on an altruistic desire to influence the lives of future medical professionals.

Attitudes of interviewers may vary from very agreeable to skeptical to openly confrontational. You may even encounter interviewers who are seemingly uninterested in process. Just remember, the interview experience is not as important to the interviewer as it is to you. While you cannot alter an interviewer's personality, you maintain the perspective that the interview is less about you personally and more about the exchange of valuable and necessary information.

The personalities and abilities of interviewers vary greatly, and you won't know who you are getting and what they are like until you get there. Accordingly, you need to be prepared to do well no matter what kind of interviewer you draw. Having gained insight into the personality types of potential interviewers from your informational interviews, you will better prepared no matter who your interviewer is.

Regrettably, the discussions about dealing with various personality types is a book unto itself and cannot be thoroughly discussed here in depth. Many great books on the subjects of dealing with difficult people and influencing the way in which you are perceived by others exist on the market. If you believed you may need a bit of help shoring up your "soft skills," you may wish to investigate these further.

Putting on Your Game Face

You make your impression from the time you walk on campus until you complete your interview. If you note each aspect of your presentation as described here before the interview, you are certain to make that impression a positive one.

Attire

The way you dress should be neat and professional. For both men and women, this requires a suit—the only appropriate dress for a formal interview.

When interviewing, you should reflect the image of someone who wants to attend a prestigious medical school. It is much safer to overdress! Your professional attire not only illustrates how serious you are in embracing a medical career, it conveys to your interviewer how much you value their time.

Body Language

Both your words and body language reflect your character and preparedness. You don't want to seem uncomfortable, unwilling to engage, or defensive in your interviews (one reason you are encouraged to practice with informational and mock interviews as much as possible). Be aware of your body language, but not overwhelmed by thinking about it.

Know the School

Before arriving for your admissions interview, investigate the academic, social, historical, and geographic features of the institution. Use the Internet and the academic catalog to get an overview of the curriculum. Since you will likely be asked (at least once) during your interview why you want to attend their school, use your research to form opinions of the most appealing features of the school and to formulate thoughtful questions specific to the academic program. Your enthusiasm, if it is sincere, will not go unnoticed. Take care during the interview to never make interviewers think their school is your second (third or fourth) choice, even if it is.

Listen

Listen carefully to the questions you are asked. Pause a moment before answering to make certain you understand the question and what information the interviewer thinks is important in your answer.

Some questions may be quite ambiguous, so if you are unclear as to what the point of the question is, be certain to gain clarification before answering. Remember the technique of responding to questions by asking questions (Chapter 5)? This is the perfect place to employ this tactic. Respond by asking whether the question they are asking pertains to your first interpretation of it or to a secondary interpretation.

For instance, if you are asked the extremely ambiguous question, "How did you get here?" You could respond, "I'm not certain that I understand the question clearly. Are you asking how I came to select the Institute of

Internal Medicine for my education, or how I came to the conclusion that I wanted to study internal medicine?" Once again, you are demonstrating an interest in the speaker by listening carefully to the questions posed while subtly exhibiting your intelligence by noting the question could have several answers.

Be Honest

Do not invent answers. If you cannot answer a question that requires information outside of your experience, simply apologize and reply that you do not know. Your interviewers know their subject matter well and will be unimpressed with too much creativity. Try to avoid hanging yourself with falsehoods or invention.

Know Your Application

Be prepared to provide details included in your application The interviewer may not be familiar with or remember the specifics. If you did research as an undergraduate, prepare clear statements of the goals and methodology of your research, identify your contribution to those goals, and why the research was important. Identify any bearing that the extracurricular activities you included in your application may have on your aptitude as a medical school student.

Types of Interviews

You may have one or several interviews in different formats.

Panel Interview

Panel interviews can be very intimidating with as many as six people asking you different questions. It will be important to acknowledge everyone in the room by making eye contact with each of the interviewers. A common mistake made by some candidates is to maintaining eye contact with only one person. While you should focus primarily on the individual who asks a question, acknowledge the other people while you speak.

Blind

In a blind interview, no personal information, application information, or academic performance has been disclosed to the interviewer. This type of interview is more likely going to address behavioral, subjective, and ethical questions. Behavioral questions ask candidates to describe a situation that prompted action and results. We will learn more about behavioral and ethical questions in Chapter 7. An example of a subjective question might be, "Tell me why you want to be a doctor?" Interviewers in blind interview sessions typically evaluate candidates on how articulately and effectively they answer questions.

Partial Blind

A partial blind interview is one in which an interviewer only has a portion of your application. The interviewer may only have your transcripts or your personal essay to use as reference. As in a blind interview, you might get asked several behavioral questions or ethical and moral questions.

Free-For-All

In a free-for-all interview, the interviewer isn't required to ask specific questions. He has access to all of your information, but may choose not to refer to it and instead just try to determine whether you can carry on a conversation that flows and stays on topic. An interviewer might start with general conversation to gauge your ability to connect with others, but if things don't go well the interviewer may resort to your file. Seize the opportunity to ask questions and engage in conversation.

Stress

In this kind of interview, the interviewer will intentionally try to put you in a corner and create stress. For example, an interviewer might ask an ethical question and then become irate at the answer and argue with you. The idea is to determine how well you maintain composure in a challenging environment.

Types of Interview Questions

Once you've completed several informational interviews, you can begin preparing specifically for your medical school interviews. By now, you have probably made all of the arrangements to show up on time, dress appropriately, and ensure you will be well-rested by the time you arrive for your interview.

Just as there are different kinds of interviews and interviewers, there are many kinds interview questions. You should be ready for them all.

Before we explore the various types of questions interviewers commonly use, be sure you are acquainted with the medical school itself. Knowing the answers to general questions about the school will help you get an overview of the type of environment they nurture and provide a level of familiarization before meeting with your interviewers. Get answers to the questions below about each of the schools at which you have interviews scheduled.

- ❏ Who is the school's current president?

- ❏ Has the school received any recent accolades?

- ❏ Who is the school's most prestigious medical professional?

- ❏ What types of research does the school perform?

- ❏ When was the school's department of medicine founded?

The types of questions interviewers will ask you include, but are not limited to, those that are general, ethical, situational, and personal. Most of your interviews will have a combination of these types of questions. There are some things that you should know about each.

General Questions

These are often fact-checking questions and warm-up questions which may include "Where did you graduate?" or "Is this your first interview of the day?" General questions often help start the conversation. It is important to keep small talk going and not say too much. This is not the time to get excited and over-divulge your personal history. In fact, there will be a time and place for everything, so don't force it.

Ethical Questions

Ethical questions may be especially challenging. An example of an ethical question is, "A group of physicians and nurses were accused of administering deadly doses of morphine to patients who were severely ill during the Hurricane Katrina evacuation. Assuming it is true, do you feel they were justified in their actions? Why or why not?"

The key to answering this type of question is to make an argument and justify your position. Be sure you understand what you are supporting and that you can defend your choices. Frequently, such questions have no obvious right or wrong answers and interviewers simply want to determine if you are capable of thinking on your feet.

Behavioral Questions

These questions are unbelievably difficult if you are not prepared. An example of a behavioral question is: "Describe a time when you were faced with a challenge and used good judgment to resolve the issue." These types of questions require you to think and it can be very difficult to know when you have offered a satisfactory answer. Many qualified candidates crack under the pressure of these questions simply because they are not prepared.

The interviewer is seeking a response that includes a description of the situation, the action you took, and the result of your actions. These responses are termed SAR responses ("SAR" stands for Situation, Action, and Result). When asked behavioral questions, formulate your answer according to this formula: (1) Identify a situation from you past that is appropriate to the question asked and note the difficulties you encountered. (2) Describe your actions in a manner that reflects that you recognized the problems you faced and how you were able to formulate a solution to those problems. (3) Briefly describe the direct results of your actions. If you feel that the experience warrants elaboration, you may share insights about what you learned from the experience with your interviewer.

We all have had such experiences by the time we might get to this stage of our lives. Be prepared for this kind of question by creating an outline of examples from your history and practicing your answers.

Personal History Questions

Interviewers generally will use personal history inquiries to learn about the different aspects of your schooling. You should be able to speak to every single thing in your personal history. If there is something in your background that may cause difficulty-perhaps you had academic difficulties and withdrew from school for a time early in college-address it honestly and show how you resolved the problem and learned from it. Don't dwell on your answer, and don't volunteer information about such circumstances unless you are asked. But be prepared with your answer.

Asking Your Own Questions

To under-emphasize this section would be doing a massive disservice to you. You have the opportunity to show your intelligence by the questions you ask. Be sure to ask your interviewer plenty of questions about the medical program, their personal experiences, and the student resources available. Asking questions during an interview makes a powerful impact, but be certain the questions you ask are relevant and significant to your prospective course of study. When posing questions to your interviewers during an actual interview, your questions can help you determine if that school is right for you. For instance, you may ask questions such as, "Does this school allow students to perform their rotations at other institutions?" Or, "Is there a mentor program available?" While these questions will do little good during a mock interview, you can keep them in mind for your medical school interviews.

Don't forget that you have a limited amount of time to make a positive impression. By asking questions yourself, you may be able to direct the conversation to situations where you produced favorable results, learned something new, or had a positive effect on someone's life. If there is something really difficult to deal with in your background, something such as an expulsion for misbehavior, then you must deal with it straightforwardly and briefly, showing how you have learned from the your mistakes and become stronger. You want to create the impression such instances are unlikely to recur.

Goal Summary Revisited

It is time in the preparation process to re-examine your goal statement from Chapter 2.

❑ Gather collected information (reading, notes from informational interviews, etc.)

❑ Compare the information you have gathered about each profession with your life goals from Chapter 2, Exploring Your Options.

❑ Discern the best education path to the profession(s) to which you are most attracted

❑ Create succinctly worded goal statements for each of your best possible career paths. Include your aspiration for that career, and how your education will help you obtain that goal.

Goal Statement

I want _____

_____

_____

_____

_____

_____

_____

Chapter 7

The Snapshot Interview

Before you can improve the quality of your answers to some basic interview questions and the confidence with which you present those answers, you will need an idea of your performance at this point. Here is a brief exercise to take a snapshot of your current skill set. A video camera or audio recorder is highly recommended for this task. We also recommended that you have someone available to act as an interviewer. This exercise is designed to provide you with a first glance at possible interview questions. This is the place from which you will gauge your progress and attempt to adapt your interviewing style.

Record yourself if possible, even if you simply use an audio recording device available through your MP3 player or computer system. Nearly all computers have basic voice recording ability. If you use a video camera, find a quiet room and set the camera so that your full body is displayed in the picture. You don't need to see the interviewer. Make sure the lighting is adequate and the audio quality is reasonable.

Give the questions from the following pages to the person playing the role of interviewer. The questions should be asked in a random order. If you are unable to find an assistant, read and answer the questions out loud as a role-playing exercise. Listen to each question, think about your response before you answer and give the best answer you can at the time.

Once your practice interview is complete, allow your interviewer a few moments to jot down her thoughts about the overall interview. The more honest your friend can be in her evaluation of your interview, the more prepared you will be for the real thing. Listen carefully to your friend's critique, then review the video or audiotape of your interview and evaluate yourself.

Practice Questions

Have the interviewer rate your answers to each question from 1 (Poor) to 5 (Excellent). Was the answer clear and informative? Note strengths and weaknesses in the candidate's interview approach. Where can improvement be made?

1. What makes you a good candidate for medical school?

   POOR `1` `2` `3` `4` `5` EXCELLENT

   Comments: _____

   _____

   _____

2. What prompted you to consider medicine as a career?

   POOR `1` `2` `3` `4` `5` EXCELLENT

   Comments: _____

   _____

   _____

3. Why would you be a good doctor?

   POOR `1` `2` `3` `4` `5` EXCELLENT

   Comments: _____

   _____

   _____

4. What does being a good doctor mean to you?

POOR 1 2 3 4 5 EXCELLENT

Comments: _____

_____

_____

5. How do you anticipate paying for medical school?

POOR 1 2 3 4 5 EXCELLENT

Comments: _____

_____

_____

6. What is your greatest weakness?

POOR 1 2 3 4 5 EXCELLENT

Comments: _____

_____

_____

7. What are your greatest strengths?

POOR 1 2 3 4 5 EXCELLENT

Comments: _____

_____

_____

8. What field of medicine interests you most?

    POOR 1 2 3 4 5 **EXCELLENT**

    Comments: _____

    _____

    _____

9. What is the purpose of a doctor?

    POOR 1 2 3 4 5 **EXCELLENT**

    Comments: _____

    _____

    _____

10. Do you have any experience in the medical field?

    POOR 1 2 3 4 5 **EXCELLENT**

    Comments: _____

    _____

    _____

11. What do you envision being your greatest challenge in study-
    ing medicine?

    POOR 1 2 3 4 5 **EXCELLENT**

    Comments: _____

    _____

    _____

12. What are your interests outside of your studies?

POOR 1 2 3 4 5 EXCELLENT

Comments: _____

_____

_____

13. Why would you like to be part of our medical program?

POOR 1 2 3 4 5 EXCELLENT

Comments: _____

_____

_____

14. Where do you see yourself in 10 years?

POOR 1 2 3 4 5 EXCELLENT

Comments: _____

_____

_____

15. What are your thoughts about genetic cloning?

POOR 1 2 3 4 5 EXCELLENT

Comments: _____

_____

_____

16. Can you describe a time when you overcame a challenging obstacle?

POOR | 1 | 2 | 3 | 4 | 5 | EXCELLENT

Comments: _____

_____

_____

17. Do you prefer working in groups or alone?

POOR | 1 | 2 | 3 | 4 | 5 | EXCELLENT

Comments: _____

_____

_____

18. Have you ever disagreed with a boss/professor, and if so, what was the outcome?

POOR | 1 | 2 | 3 | 4 | 5 | EXCELLENT

Comments: _____

_____

_____

19. Who is your role model?

POOR | 1 | 2 | 3 | 4 | 5 | EXCELLENT

Comments: _____

_____

_____

20. Envisioning yourself as a physician, how do you plan on handling patients' belief systems that are not in accordance with your own?

POOR `1` `2` `3` `4` `5` EXCELLENT

Comments: _____

_____

_____

Reviewer: How would your rate the candidate's overall performance? Were the answers confident and clear? Did the candidate appear to be enthusiastic about the answers he/she gave? Which aspects of delivery were executed well? Which weren't?

POOR `1` `2` `3` `4` `5` EXCELLENT

Comments: _____

_____

_____

_____

_____

_____

_____

_____

_____

_____

Chapter 8

Mock Interview Challenge

Throughout the previous chapters you have been discovering that interviewing is a skill that demands your focus be divided between presentation of yourself and the intent of your interviewer, all while attempting to speak earnestly about your motivations and desires. Hopefully, all of the information you have acquired (your research into prospective fields of study, conversations and interviews with medical practitioners, and deep introspection about the impetus behind your goals) have helped you form a decisive image of yourself in your chosen roles as both medical student and, eventually, professional. You should be able to answer most general questions about the choice you have made to enter medical school and what you hope to achieve by pursing a degree in medicine.

At this stage, you must practice conveying your aspirations and knowledge to others in a way that is both cogent and sincere. As has been noted previously, the more you exercise your interviewing skills in different situations, the more attentive you will be to the subtle details of each aspect of your interview.

The foundation of the medical school interview is primarily a social one. You will be inspected for your suitability as a medical student (or researcher, doctor, educator). This is a purely subjective experience for the interviewer. The biases and preconceptions the interviewer possesses will be fundamentally unknown to you, so your ambition during the interview should be two-fold: (1) present yourself as a competent and successful person, and (2) employ listening and questioning skills learned in previous chapters to develop a positive personal relationship with the interviewer. These goals, you may recognize, have little to do with what you know or your desire for a medical degree. Although the topic of conversation will primarily be about your potential as student, the situation is actually designed so that the interviewer(s) can learn more about who you are from interacting with you face-to-face.

One of the best ways to prepare for any social situation (particularly a situation that is potentially quite stressful) is by role-playing. For that reason, the final stage of preparation is the mock interview. This popular teaching method reinforces good habits in a relatively safe environment, giving you the opportunity to sharpen some of the skills you have learned during your informational interviews, You may already have experience with role-playing in other situations. If so, this chapter will simply outline ways to employ this tool for your admissions interviews.

When you walk into your medical school interview, you will want to present yourself in a way that will separate you from everyone else, exuding confidence and with so much momentum that the interviewers will be moved to respond. If you approach the practice exercises from this book seriously, the responses you receive will be overwhelmingly positive.

Informal Mock Interview

Attempt as many of these practice rounds as you can arrange. Employ the assistance of a few friends or relatives to act as "interviewers." Have your assistant ask you as many as 25 of the practice questions provided in Appendix A at random. The interview should take approximately one hour.

Your friend should attempt to devise questions that present themselves from your answers; this will allow you to practice impromptu responses for questions you perhaps have not considered. If you can, conduct several mock interviews with more than one person, having each spontaneously ask questions during the interview.

These first practice interviews can be less formal than the final mock interview (Chapter 9). You don't have to wear interview attire and they can happen on the spur of the moment, whenever you can arrange to conduct them. Even though they will not be terribly formal, it will be a good idea to videotape your mock interviews so you can evaluate your performance and progress. Use the recommendations from Chapter 7, The Snapshot Interview, for taping your mock interviews.

As will be the case in the actual medical school interview, your mock interviews are a bit different from informational interviews in that you will not have as much control over the interview, so you be prepared to answer many different questions. This kind of practice will help you become comfortable with the inevitable pressures of the real interview.

Once you feel comfortable with your performance in these informal mock interviews, test yourself by stepping up the challenge with a formal mock interview. In the next chapter you will be given instructions for arranging a formal mock interview, but very little additional recommendations. Be warned, that exercise will be difficult to pull off without indulging the desire to "cheat" a bit, but if you are able to do so, you will gain a great deal of insight about your preparedness for the admissions interview.

Review

Taking the time to do a quick review of your tapes is important. You can either take a look at the end of all of the mock interviews, or review your progress along the way. The most apparent differences will be noticeable in the answers to your questions, which should reflect an evolving perspective. Body language and ability to speak confidently should improve dramatically as well, noticeably from tape to tape.

If you review the footage and find do not detect the improvements that you feel are necessary, engage more fully in the informational interview process. Practice will help calm your nerves and attune your perspective with your delivery.

Chapter 9

Formal Mock Interview

This final stage of preparation for your admissions interview will prove to be the most demanding and the most rewarding.

The first thing you will need to do is acquire the aid of an assistant. The ideal circumstance would be for you to enlist the help of someone who understands the complexity and import of your upcoming interview, perhaps a medical professional who personally has undergone the academic admissions process. Acquiring the assistance of such a person may prove to be difficult or impossible for many reasons. If so, do not forego the practice. Ask someone close to you. The only requirement is that you ask a mature individual, someone who is invested in your future and has some career experience. Call on your family and friends if need be. Some of them will be glad to help because they already believe in you.

Introduce the goal and concept of the mock interview as described in Chapter 8. Explain to your assistant that you need help setting up a mock interview as a formal practice for your admissions interview.

IMPORTANT — The integrity of the interview is dependent on the assumption that you have not read Appendix B. Simply hand this book over to your assistant instructing them to go to Appendix B.

Attach a calendar of your schedule for the next four weeks listing all of the times when you will be occupied with work or classes or times when you will be out of town. No other commitments should interfere with your availability. The calendar should also include your name, phone number, and e-mail address.

Once you have handed the book over, you will wait for a call from your interviewer. You are obligated to meet at whatever time the interviewer specifies, regardless of what you have to do to get there. It doesn't matter where or when he or she says, since you will have to make the same concessions for your admissions interview.

Notes on Mock Interviewing

Take the mock interview very seriously. Prepare as you would for your actual medical school interview. As you go to the mock interview, imagine that you are walking into the real thing. Imagine the surroundings as

a real school, even if it is your living room. Wear the clothing that you will be wearing for your admissions interview.

Note 1: During your mock interviews, questioning an interviewer during the mock interview is encouraged only if your inquiries can be reasonably answered. Obviously, if the interviewer is a friend who is not a medical professional, there will be few opportunities to ask questions that are field-specific. You don't expect them to answer, you just want to practice asking those questions. Primarily, you want focus on integrating your experiences from the informational interviews into your responses. Have you talked about your experience as part of your answer? Your goal is to use the knowledge you have already gathered to establish yourself as a candidate who takes the medical profession seriously.

Note 2: Asking the interviewer mock questions about your prospective school will not benefit you tremendously here, but let the interviewer know beforehand that you will attempt to interject questions just as you would during your real interview. The interviewer should be prepared for this.

Asking for Professional Assistance

Doctors are generally very busy people. Requesting them to invest several hours of their time or recruit other professionals to gather for a mock interview may not be practical. If you would like a medical professional to coordinate the mock interview panel, you may want use the following sample letters as a guides in making your request.

Informal Request

Dear *Name*:

I am contacting you because I need your help. As you may know, I am trying my best to prepare for my medical school interviews. Mock interviews will help me practice my interview skills. I am going to provide you with some mock interview tools that will serve as a guide to establishing a very realistic interview scenario. There are going to be very specific instructions that you will be asked to follow. I am asking you now for your help.

Our effort will help me prepare for my upcoming medical school interviews. I want to make a great impression, and I think your assistance would be invaluable. Please consider when you will have time available and get back to me. I'll make my schedule fit your schedule. We can do the practice interview at any location that is convenient to you, or I can arrange a space. It can be any time during the next month. Again, thank you in advance, as I know this is a lot to ask of you.

Sincerely,

Jill James

Formal Request

When asking someone whom you do not know well to help you prepare by conducting and organizing a mock interview, this letter or something similar may be helpful.

Dear *Name*:

You may recall we met on (date) to briefly discuss my interest in your discipline as a possible concentration in medical school. I am now at the point of preparing for my medical school interviews and would like to have a mock interview conducted in the most authentic way possible. Would you be willing to help? The interview can take place at a time and place convenient for you. If you do not have a suggestion about place, I can arrange a setting, but that is up to you. If you think it possible to enlist one or more of your colleagues in the process, that would make it even more realistic. The only restriction is that the mock interview take place within the next (however many) weeks.

Thank you for considering my request. I am aware it involves a considerable investment of time and energy and will understand if you are not able to participate in this manner.

Sincerely,

Jack Johnson

Chapter 10

Conclusion

Good luck!

If you have taken the time to follow this guide, you have already started to reap the benefits of building your interview skills. If, however, you've read this book without truly participating in the processes it details, this exercise will have done very little for you.

Attempt to assess your progress. Ask yourself these questions:

❑ Can I see myself in the roles I have chosen as medical student, graduate, and medical professional?

❑ Do I feel better prepared to meet my future?

❑ Am I at ease with the idea of meeting complete strangers who hold the keys to that future?

If you sense that you are unprepared in any way, persist in practicing the interview skills outlined in the previous chapters until all the aspects of interviewing feel ordinary and not in the least bit threatening. Rigorous repetition is essential to becoming comfortable in any situation. Placing yourself in situations which mimic the admissions interview offers you the chance to become more at ease when faced with the actual event.

In addition, try to understand the motivations of your interviewers. The more you understand what they are seeking from you, the better prepared you will be to answer their questions in a manner that allows your talents and personality to shine through. Your own motivations are equally important. The more keenly you perceive your goals, the more conviction and confidence you will demonstrate when your motivations for those goals are examined.

You've worked diligently to get to this point and have prepared for the hard work that will be demanded of you in the near future. Take a deep breath, relax, and enjoy your interviews! You're ready!

Appendix A

Snapshot Interview Questions

1. Why do you want to be a doctor?

2. What will you do if you aren't accepted to medical school?

3. What is your favorite part of our program?

4. Is there a good deal of drug use at your school? Possible follow up: Have you taken drugs?

5. Which languages do you speak? Why?

6. Which of your college courses interested you the most?

7. What is your greatest weakness?

8. What makes you special?

9. What do you do to relax?

10. What are the qualities of a good doctor?

11. What is your favorite fiction book?

12. What is your favorite movie?

13. Why isn't your GPA higher?

14. What do you want to be in 10 years?

15. What are your career goals?

16. What area would you like to specialize in? Why?

17. What are your thoughts on universal health care?

18. What will you contribute to the health care industry to make it better?

19. Tell me about a challenge that you have overcome?

20. What do you find really exciting about medicine?

21. What do you find really boring about medicine?

22. How successful do you think you've been so far?

23. What do you think it takes to be successful in medical school?

24. What do you know about this organization?

25. How much money do you think you will make when you graduate?

26. Tell me about the three accomplishments of which you are most proud?

27. What experience have you had managing others?

28. What motivates you to put forth your best effort?

29. What are the kinds of things you are most confident doing?

30. What is something that makes you angry? How do you deal with it?

31. What do you think will be your greatest challenge in completing medical school or learning how to be a doctor?

32. In your view, what is the most pressing problem facing medicine today?

33. How will you pay for medical school?

34. If you could go back, how would you have prepared better academically?

35. Tell me about yourself.

36. Do you have any hobbies or leisure activities?

37. What do you feel are the most important qualities in being a good doctor?

38. Why would you be a good doctor?

39. Would you consider yourself to be a leader or a follower? How do you know this about yourself?

40. What problems do you see in patient care?

41. What problems do you see with the admissions process?

42. What is your focus? Why did you choose it?

43. What non-science courses did you like the most?

44. What can be done about rising health care costs?

45. What will you find most difficult about medical school? How will you handle that?

46. What are your strong points? What are your weaknesses?

47. What has been your biggest failure and how did you handle it?

48. How do you feel about animal research?

49. Do you work well under pressure? Give an example. What, in hindsight, were you most dissatisfied with about your performance? What did you learn from your experience?

50.   What exposure have you had to the medical profession?

51.   Tell me about your research.

52.   Discuss your clinical experiences.

53.   Discuss your volunteer work.

54.   What do you think you will like most about medicine?

55.   What do you think you will like least about medicine?

56.   Why do you think our school is a good fit for you?

57.   What are three things you want to change about yourself?

58.   How would you describe the relationship between science and medicine?

59.   Which family member has most influenced you so far and why?

60.   Where do you see yourself in ten years?

61.   How do you see the field of medicine changing in the next ten years? How do you see yourself fitting into those changes?

62.   Tell me about yourself.

63.   Have you looked at our program and the school? What do you like about it? What don't you like about it?

64.   Why choose medicine over some other career?

65. What field of medicine interests you most?

66. What have you done that shows initiative? What did you gain from that experience? How were you most/least satisfied with that endeavor?

67. How do you respond to criticism? Describe a situation where your work was criticized. What was your immediate reaction to the situation?

68. How do you respond to personal conflicts with others? Describe how you successfully resolved a conflict with someone else.

69. Describe a typical day from your elementary school days.

70. What questions do you have for me about our school?

71. Name some strategies to address the problem of smoking among teens; talk about some that haven't been tried.

72. How would your best friend convince me I should admit you to our medical school?

73. If you could be any character in history, who would it be? Why?

74. How did you decide to apply to our medical school?

75. Why did you choose our specific program?

76. Would you perform abortions as a doctor? Under what conditions?

77. Name an accomplishment you are most proud of.

78. What do you think is wrong with the current health care system in the US? Do you have any ideas how these issues could be fixed?

79. Identify a meaningful experience you've had and how it shaped you to pursue work as a physician.

80. In your present living situation, how do you settle disputes with your roommates?

81. What interests you outside of medicine and getting into medical school?

82. What would you bring to this school?

83. What was your favorite class? Least favorite? Why?

84. When did you decide to pursue medicine?

85. What would you do if you weren't accepted?

86. How do you feel about the prospect of a career that spans 20 or 30 years?

87. How did you study for MCAT?

88. What do you like best about the field of medicine?

89. Do you have any volunteer experience?

90. What is the most difficult situation/biggest challenge you have faced?

91. What leadership experience do you have?

92. Do you think you could complete your coursework with a family?

93. What do you feel makes you a competitive student?

94. What specialties have you considered and why?

95. What do you want the admissions committee to know about you that's not in your file?

96. What have you done to show you have manual dexterity?

97. Tell me about yourself.

98. Describe your family.

99. What community service have you performed?

100. Why should we accept you over another student with the same qualifications?

101. What is the future of medicine?

102. How do your values fit with the medical profession?

103. What makes you unique?

104. Where do you see yourself in ten years?

105. What do you do if your best friend wanted to copy your assignment?

106. How would you feel about treating a patient with AIDS?

107. What do you do if you are not accepted this year?

108. Which preliminary courses did you decide to avoid and why?

109. If you were a tree what kind of tree would you be?

110. Describe yourself in three words.

111. If you were interviewing me what would you ask? Why?

112. What is your purpose in life?

113. What do you think about affirmative action?

114. If you could invite 3 people to dinner who would they be? Why?

115. Name 5 countries and capitols in Europe.

116. Whom do you admire the most and why?

117. Have you ever taken illegal drugs?

118. What have you done to show that you like the medical field?

119. How would you be a good fit for our school?

Appendix B

Formal Mock Interview

Do NOT read the following pages if you are
Medical School Candidate

Provide the entire appended document and
cover letter to designated interviewer.

Do Not Peek

Dear Sir or Madam:

Someone who trusts you has presented you with this letter and attached outline for organizing a mock interview. If you would be willing to expend a modicum of effort and some of your valuable time in this endeavor, you will be preparing a candidate for medical school for one of the most important days of his or her life. It has taken dedication for the student to reach this significant point, and your assistance would be immeasurably appreciated.

What you are being asked to do is rather straightforward: without the student's foreknowledge, plan a mock medical school interview designed to simulate the stressful conditions the candidate will face in his or her admissions interview. You can help this candidate walk into an admissions interview with experience they could not otherwise obtain. You may orchestrate this mock interview as you see fit, using the guidelines presented here. The exercise as it is laid out here will be the ultimate role-playing rehearsal for interview preparation.

Thank you, in advance, for your willingness to participate in this endeavor.

Part 1. Personnel

The first task in planning the mock interview includes a bit of trickery.

The doctor-to-be probably assumes that you will conduct the interview. Ideally, this is not true; instead, you will only organize the event and will not be present during the interview itself. Find up to three people with whom the student is not acquainted, removing the comfort of familiarity from the proceedings. Members of your family or a friends or colleagues will suffice. Ideal candidates for the job of interviewer are people who perform this role in real life: a human resources representative, office manager, academic committee member, etc., anyone who must evaluate performance and suitability of individuals for any task. The more experience, the better. An appropriate choice on your part will be someone who is willing to dedicate a couple of hours in preparation and spend a couple of hours interviewing.

You may find it easier to introduce the concept to prospective candidates by e-mail. Attached you will find a form letter you can use or adapt as you see fit for that purpose.

Dear *Name*:

I have been asked to help (*Candidate's Name*) prepare for (his/her) medical school interview. Part of that process is to conduct a mock interview of one hour with real medical professionals who understand just how important these interviews are. I have met this young person and believe my assistance is warranted because of (his/her) character and zeal in preparation. Would you be willing to meet with us on (*day / date / place / time range*) to explore this. I would appreciate it and so would this worthy candidate?

If you can participate, please let me know by (date), and I will provide a list of sample questions that you can use or expand upon as is your preference. In addition, I will provide a copy of the candidate's resume and one of the applications completed for medical school that you can use in guiding your preparation. I know this involves some real effort on your part, but I believe it is justified by the possible gains to the profession represented by this candidate.

Thank you for considering this request. I earnestly hope you can join us.

Sincerely,

Signature

Part 2. Location

Establish a location in which to conduct the interview, preferably a place where the interviewee has never been (an office setting, or, if you prefer somewhere less distracting, another person's home). Attempt to incite discomfort by removing the candidate from familiar surroundings.

The interviewee has been instructed to answer your call from the telephone number given and to commit to whatever time you set forth. The schedules of the interviewers should take precedent. The interviewee's role is to show up where and when asked just as they would for their admissions interview.

Ultimately, the goal is to make the conditions as close to the real interview as possible. Request the interviewers to dress appropriately; professional attire is recommended. Food or drink should not be offered prior to the evaluation phase. The candidate should be seated apart from the interviewers.

Recording the interview for the candidate to review later may be extremely useful in a performance review. If you decide to use a video camera, be certain to test video and audio quality beforehand to be certain your location has adequate lighting and the interviewer can be heard clearly in recording.

The last requirement for this exercise is that all interviewers have a note pad or a clipboard for notes. Stopping to write comments between questions also adds an element of stress, because the interviewee will wonder what is being written.

Part 3. Preparation

Work together with the potential interviewer(s) to structure the interview. If you know the candidate well, attempt to focus on questions in areas about which the interviewee is concerned. Use this information to test him or her under pressure!

Attached to this document, you find a list of interview questions. Creating your own questions should not be necessary but is acceptable if you chose to personalize the experience. Each interviewer should have a copy of the questions that will be asked. Interviewers should review questions before meeting with the medical school candidate. Order is irrelevant.

Instruct your interviewer(s) to be as demanding as they feel comfortable. The process should be taken quite seriously, since the interviewee will gain nothing without a degree of pressure. Always encourage a tough (even curt), but cordial, approach. Individuals who take the role of interviewers may show disinterest in the candidate's answers should the responses to their questions be uninformative, bland, or rambling. Contrarily, the interviewers may exhibit positive body language if the interviewee is doing well. This will mimic elements that will be present in the real interview.

Part 4. Grading

Rate the answers given to each question from 1 (Poor) to 5 (Excellent). A higher score should be given if the candidate mentions facts to support answers, such as recent research and experiences. A lower score should be given for responses which are wholly inappropriate or irrelevant.

Interviewers should grade based on how effectively and articulately the medical school candidate answers questions. Thus, each interviewer should attempt to critique each answer objectively and dispassionately, taking note of anything that stands out as brilliant or possibly problematic. These notes offer the medical school candidate the best opportunity to improve their interviewing skills.

Although subjective, the scoring should guide the interviewers to focus their feedback. Please note that the score of the interview is secondary to the situational exposure. Although much emphasis will be placed on the score, the experience of interviewing is where the real benefit lies.

General questions should be judged on the candidate's ability to answer clearly and honestly. Behavioral questions should be judged on how effectively the interviewee describes a situation, the action taken, and its end result. Ethical questions should be rated on how well the candidate states his position and explains the basis for his stance. Interviewers should not penalize an ethical position solely on the basis that it is not in alignment with their own. Again, objectivity should be the primary goal of the interviewers.

While grading responses, the score should be lowered if the interviewee exhibits any of the following behavior:

- ❑ Muttering
- ❑ Mumbling
- ❑ Saying 'um'
- ❑ Rambling
- ❑ Refusing to answer a question

- ❑ Defensiveness
- ❑ Does not maintain eye contact
- ❑ Poor posture

Do Not Peek

Overall score should be reduced if the candidate arrives late, is not professionally dressed, does not greet each of the interviewers in turn upon arrival, or does anything inappropriate for an interviewing environment (such as neglecting to turn off a cell phone or bringing a friend).

The interview should be limited to one hour.

Questions 1–11: General Questions

Answers should be mature, honest and demonstrate thoughtfulness.

1. Why do you want to be a doctor?

   POOR 1 2 3 4 5 EXCELLENT

   Comments: _____

   _____

   _____

2. Tell me about yourself.

   POOR 1 2 3 4 5 EXCELLENT

   Comments: _____

   _____

   _____

3. How will you pay for medical school?

   POOR 1 2 3 4 5 EXCELLENT

   Comments: _____

   _____

   _____

4. What do you think will be your greatest challenge in completing medical school or learning how to be a doctor?

   POOR 1 2 3 4 5 EXCELLENT

   Comments: _____

   _____

   _____

5.   In your view, what is the most pressing problem facing medicine today?

POOR `1` `2` `3` `4` `5` EXCELLENT

Comments: _____

_____

_____

6.   What are your two best points?

POOR `1` `2` `3` `4` `5` EXCELLENT

Comments: _____

_____

_____

7.   What are your two weakest points?

POOR `1` `2` `3` `4` `5` EXCELLENT

Comments: _____

_____

_____

8.   If you could do anything different in your education, what would you do?

POOR `1` `2` `3` `4` `5` EXCELLENT

Comments: _____

_____

_____

9.   To what other schools are you applying?

POOR `1` `2` `3` `4` `5` EXCELLENT

Comments: _____

_____

_____

10.   Why do you think our school is a good fit for you?

POOR 1 2 3 4 5 EXCELLENT

Comments: _____

_____

_____

11.   Is the school that you are interviewing at right now your first
choice? Scoring Guide: If candidate indicates that your school is
not his or her first choice, give 0 points.

POOR 1 2 3 4 5 EXCELLENT

Comments: _____

_____

_____

Questions 12-14: Behavioral Questions

Answers should be descriptive of the Situation presented by the question,
the Action taken by the interviewee and the Result of the actions (SAR).
These are often considered the most challenging questions to answer.

12.   Describe a time when you were faced with a stressful situation
that demonstrated your coping skills.

POOR 1 2 3 4 5 EXCELLENT

Comments: _____

_____

_____

13. Give me a specific example of a time when you used good judgment and logic in solving a problem.

POOR | 1 | 2 | 3 | 4 | 5 | EXCELLENT

Comments: _____

_____

_____

14. Give me an example of a time when you set a goal and were able to meet or achieve it.

POOR | 1 | 2 | 3 | 4 | 5 | EXCELLENT

Comments: _____

_____

_____

Questions 15 through 19: Ethical Questions

Points are accrued when answers are logical and concise. The candidate should not be penalized for answers that differ from your beliefs; however, answers must be clearly communicated.

15. What are your opinions on abortion?

POOR | 1 | 2 | 3 | 4 | 5 | EXCELLENT

Comments: _____

_____

_____

16. What are your opinions on euthanasia?

POOR 1 2 3 4 5 EXCELLENT

Comments: _____

_____

_____

17. What are your opinions on HMOs?

POOR 1 2 3 4 5 EXCELLENT

Comments: _____

_____

_____

18. Tell me what you think about cloning?

POOR 1 2 3 4 5 EXCELLENT

Comments: _____

_____

_____

19. How far do you believe a doctor's responsibility extends to his or

her patients?

POOR 1 2 3 4 5 EXCELLENT

Comments: _____

_____

_____

Questions 20-22: Personal Statements

Personal statement questions are derived from the candidate's application. Responses should coincide with the candidate's application.

20.   Tell me about your personal statement.

POOR 1 2 3 4 5 EXCELLENT

Comments: _____

_____

_____

21.   Explain your motivation to seek a career in medicine.

POOR 1 2 3 4 5 EXCELLENT

Comments: _____

_____

_____

22.   Discuss your philosophy of the medical profession and indicate your goals relevant to the profession.

POOR 1 2 3 4 5 EXCELLENT

Comments: _____

_____

_____

Final Scoring

Total Score of Interview is:

< 70:   Needs improvement in several key areas.

70-84:   Responses were adequate; neutral impression of candidate.

85-94:   Responses were delivered professionally and confidently; positive impression was achieved.

95-110: Candidate was well-prepared and organized; answers appeared genuine and logical thought was expressed.

Overall, the candidate showed exceptional:

Overall, the candidate has an opportunity to improve:

Comments:

_____

_____

_____

_____

_____

_____

_____

Debriefing

Once interviews are complete and immediate feedback has been presented, sit down with the subject and watch the interviews. Talk about what the impression the candidate made or provide commentary on what you see. Having insight into the process and taking away the mystery is part of the interview preparation. Tension is a key element in adequate preparation, but truly understanding the process will inspire confidence in the candidate during the real interview.

THANK YOU!

Made in the USA
Lexington, KY
28 August 2011